Stubby and the Puppy Pack

Books by Nikki Wallace

Stubby and the Puppy Pack

Available from MINSTREL Books

Books by Carol and Bill Wallace

The Flying Flea, Callie, and Me
That Furball Puppy and Me

Available from MINSTREL Books

Books by Bill Wallace

Red Dog
Trapped in Death Cave

Available from ARCHWAY Paperbacks

The Backward Bird Dog
Beauty
The Biggest Klutz in Fifth Grade
Blackwater Swamp
Buffalo Gal
The Christmas Spurs
Danger in Quicksand Swamp
Danger on Panther Peak
    (*Original title:* Shadow on the Snow)
A Dog Called Kitty
Eye of the Great Bear
Ferret in the Bedroom, Lizards in the Fridge
The Final Freedom
Journey into Terror
Never Say Quit
Snot Stew
Totally Disgusting!
True Friends
Upchuck and the Rotten Willy
Upchuck and the Rotten Willy: The Great Escape
Watchdog and the Coyotes

Available from MINSTREL Books

Nikki Wallace

Stubby and the Puppy Pack

Illustrated by John Steven Gurney

Nevada Public Library

A MINSTREL® HARDCOVER
PUBLISHED BY POCKET BOOKS

New York   London   Toronto   Sydney   Tokyo   Singapore

A MINSTREL HARDCOVER

A Minstrel Book published by
POCKET BOOKS, a division of Simon & Schuster Inc.
1230 Avenue of the Americas, New York, NY 10020

Text copyright © 1999 by Nikki Wallace
Illustrations copyright © 1999 by John Steven Gurney

ISBN: 0-671-02588-0

First Minstrel Books hardcover printing November 1999

10 9 8 7 6 5 4 3 2 1

A MINSTREL BOOK and colophon are registered trademarks
of Simon & Schuster Inc.

Printed in the U.S.A.

To my wonderful husband, Jon-Ed. Thank you for all your love and support, and for helping me develop the idea for this story.

and

To my parents, Carol and Bill Wallace, for sharing their love of writing and teaching me the joys that a good book can bring. Thanks for your guidance in helping me complete this book.

Stubby and the Puppy Pack

CHAPTER 1

"Ready or not, here I come."

I turned around, searching the yard with my eyes, my tail flicking back and forth. Behind me was the gray brick house where Teebo and his people lived. As I looked, I thought about some of Teebo's favorite hiding places. Starting with the garden near the back porch, I quickly took in all my surroundings. I glanced at the fish pond in the right corner of the yard. It was one of the places he liked to hide. I think the reason he enjoyed it so much was that I always slipped on the mossy rocks when I chased him there. For some reason, he thought it was funny to see me stumble. Teebo's next favorite place was the oak tree in the corner near the fence. The wooden fence divided Teebo's yard from the neighbor's. The tree there was really big, with lots of good branches to hide in. My final glance was toward the big, boxlike air conditioner near the house. That was Teebo's favorite place. Well, it was until I figured out he was always there when it was his turn to hide. He would stay there until I checked the garden, then he would sneak off into the flowers and I would never know he had been behind the air conditioner. I found him one day trying to crawl into the garden. I guess he didn't realize I was watching from behind one of the big rocks near the pond. He hasn't used the air conditioner as a hiding place since then.

Without wasting much time, I took a quick look at the shed near the oak tree. It was a small building made out of tin. Usually, I could hear his claws scratching on the metal if he was hiding on top of it. I held my breath, listening. I couldn't hear a thing. Next, I looked at the door. It was open, but not wide enough for Teebo to squeeze inside. If he was in the bushes between the shed and the oak tree, I would have to go closer to see. I could save that for last.

When I finished looking around the yard, I trotted to the flower garden near the back porch. I looked closely at the long blades of monkey grass that stood tall along the border of the flower bed. If Teebo were hiding there, the grass would be moving. Although we were both good at hiding, for some reason Teebo couldn't hold still if he hid in the monkey grass. His fluffy gray tail would twitch and cause the long slender blades to move. Today, the grass was motionless. To be safe, I ran behind the air conditioner to make sure he wasn't back there. I found nothing. No paw prints or smells.

In the corner of the yard, a flash of light caught my eye. It was sunlight reflecting off the fish pond. That was our favorite place to hunt. We would crouch down behind the rocks that surrounded the water and wait. If we were quick, we could catch the goldfish that Teebo's Daddy People put in there. We would reach into the cool water and pull them out onto the rocks. Sometimes we would eat them, but mostly we would just let them wiggle themselves back into the pond. When I reached the edge of the water, I couldn't resist looking in at all the gold specks that were swimming amongst the red and yellow water lilies. They were dodging in and out of the rocks and skimming over the green moss that lined the bottom of the pond. *Today would be a good day to catch those little guys,* I thought to myself. Quietly, I inched my way around the huge red slippery rocks. I checked behind each one and even checked between them. Teebo was not hiding anywhere near the water.

I started for the back side of the pond near the neighbor's fence. As I rounded the corner, I heard a loud commotion coming from the other side of the yard. The leaves on the giant oak tree were shaking wildly and the limbs were bouncing up and down. I stretched my neck out as far as I could, hoping to see what was going on. Cautiously, I crept closer to the tree.

"Teebo, is that you making all that noise up there?" I asked.

The tree just kept shaking and the only noise I could hear was a chattering sound. It got louder and louder as I eased my way to the oak tree.

"Teebo, I sure hope that's not you, because if it is, you're not hiding very well."

I kept watching the limbs for Teebo. When I got close enough to see, I noticed a big bird's nest made of twigs and straw. Mama Squirrel was chunking huge acorns at the nest. Actually, most of them were falling to the ground, but I knew she was aiming at the pile of twigs.

I felt my whiskers twitch. *I bet he's hiding in the nest.*

When I noticed that the pile of twigs and straw was almost in the "forbidden" branches, I decided Teebo was probably somewhere else. Quickly, I took another look around the yard to see if he had come out of some other hiding place. When there was no sign of him, I turned my attention back to the tree.

The squirrel moved closer to the nest. Her gray tail twitched. I heard my teeth grind together inside my head. *Teebo was up there. How dare he hide so close to the forbidden branches.* Mama Squirrel held a big acorn with both paws. Her tail flipped. Chattering as loud and mean as she could, she threw it. I heard the *thunk* it made when it hit Teebo's head.

"That's it," he screeched. Teebo exploded from the pile of twigs. "I've had it with you!"

Teebo shot up the tree after Mama Squirrel. She chattered and took off. Hot on her bushy tail, he chased her to the very top, then down to the very bottom. There, Mama Squirrel ran circles around and around the base of the tree. Teebo raced round and round, close behind her. They were circling the tree so fast that my eyes almost crossed as I watched.

It was hilarious. I couldn't keep from laughing.

"I'm gonna get you." Teebo hissed. "Who do you think you are, anyway?"

He stopped for a second to catch his breath. Mama Squirrel chattered, scolded, and darted back up the tree. Teebo took off after her again. She slowed down just enough to let him think he had her, then shot out of reach once more.

I laughed harder. I laughed until my sides

hurt. I flopped over on my side and rolled in the grass.

Suddenly the fur on my back stood up. Mama Squirrel was crossing the forbidden branches!

I couldn't believe it when Teebo chased after her.

My eyes flashed wide. Terrified, I put my paws over them so I wouldn't have to look. Only, after a second, I peeked.

They were running all over the bad branches. The branches over Max's yard. The branches we promised *never* to play on.

"Teebo, stop! It's not funny anymore!"

Teebo kept right on chasing the squirrel.

"You're on the forbidden branches. Quit! Come down here and leave her alone!"

I tried everything to get my friend to stop, but he wouldn't listen. He didn't even miss a stride. Finally I buried my head in my paws and tried to ignore what was happening. Maybe he was doing this to me on purpose. He wasn't going to scare me. Not this time. I just wouldn't watch.

I kept my eyes covered, until . . .

The sound of a limb cracking came from above my head. Eyes wide, I peered up into the tree. I saw Teebo falling. The breath caught in my throat. Frantically, Teebo grabbed for limbs with his front paws. He hit one branch but slipped and fell to another. Again, he missed that one.

Finally his claws caught. There, his gray body dangled over Max's yard. I couldn't swallow the lump in my throat as I watched him sway back and forth over the fence that separated good from evil.

"Hold on, Teebo!" I meowed as I watched my friend fight for his life.

That limb snapped too. I turned away. I couldn't bear to watch.

My best friend was gone—forever!

CHAPTER 2

Slowly I opened my eyes. I looked toward the tree. Breathing a sigh of relief, I realized Teebo had landed on our side of the fence.

"Whew, that was close," he said.

"Are you OK?" I asked.

"Yeah, but one of these days I'm going to get that squirrel. What makes her think that nest is hers anyway? It was a perfectly good hiding place, and she had to go and give me away. She couldn't just let me sit there. I wasn't bothering her and I wasn't trying to steal her acorns. What would I do with acorns anyway?"

I leaned closer to him and looked him in the eye.

"Are you sure you're okay?"

"Yeah." Teebo shrugged his fur.

"Good!" I snarled.

With that, I turned my back on him, stuck my nose in the air, and walked toward the flower garden. I could hear Teebo's feet hitting the hard ground as he chased after me.

"Let's play tag; you're it," he said as he swatted my side and took off.

I didn't chase him like normal, didn't even look at him, just kept walking.

"Kikki, what's wrong with you?"

I didn't answer.

"I know I got on the forbidden branches and that automatically made me it. I tagged you, so now you're it. Come and get me."

I turned and glared at him. Without a warning, I sprang into the air and hit Teebo square in the side. For a few seconds, Teebo didn't fight. When he finally realized I was being mean, he swatted back at me. I rolled him a couple of times across the yard. We were hissing and spitting so much that we sounded like My Carol's dishwasher.

"Kikki, stop, that hurts. What's wrong with you? Why are you so mad?"

I quit fighting with him and walked over to the monkey grass to lie down. I didn't look at Teebo or say a word to him.

"Hey," he said. "Are you mad at me, or do you just not like me anymore?"

Teebo bowed his head low and plopped down by the pansies on the far side of the garden. His bottom lip was sticking out and his eyes were droopy when he looked over at me.

"I'm sorry, Teebo. You just scared me really bad. You know we promised never to go on the forbidden branches. What were you doing? You were chasing that squirrel all over the tree, not even paying attention. I could just imagine that big, ugly, mean Max standing on the other side of the fence, his mouth watering, just waiting for you to fall into his yard. Then what? That's right, I'd never see my best friend again. You're my best friend in the whole world, and I just don't know what I'd do without you."

"Well, I'm sorry too, but best friends don't hit with their claws out."

"I didn't mean to hurt you. I was just scared."

Teebo stood up and arched his back. He walked over and sat beside me.

"Well, cheer up, Stubby," he said as he swatted one of my ears.

Teebo knew he was the only one who could get away with calling me Stubby. It was okay for him to say it, but if anyone else called me Stubby, I got really mad. Teebo did too. He never let anyone make fun of me.

I tried to smile at him, but I was still feeling kind of hurt.

Staying low to the ground, Teebo leaned around to look me in the eye.

"I'm really sorry," he said. "I know I scared you. I didn't mean to upset you like that. You're my best friend too." He reached over my back with his paw. With a big squeeze, Teebo gave me a hug.

"You're it!" Teebo shouted as he sped across the yard. He headed for the garden pond. I almost caught him, but the slippery rocks made my feet spin out of control. My paws were moving, but the rest of me stayed in one place.

"Come on, Kikki, you can run faster than

that." Teebo laughed as he stood on the biggest rock at the back of the pond.

When I finally quit slipping and sliding, I chased him to the shed. Teebo nudged the door open with his head and darted inside. We made a lot of noise as we zipped around the shelves and dodged between the tools on the floor. We knocked over the broom, the rake, several of his Mama People's garden tools, and the big metal trash can she uses while cleaning the yard. I finally tagged Teebo when he tried to jump out the door. He jumped low, and I hit his back paw with my front one.

"You're it now," I said. I took off for the oak tree. He followed close behind me. Teebo was faster than me, but I had some pretty good moves. I made my way around the yard, darting in and out of the bushes that lined my trail to the giant oak tree. I let Teebo chase me a couple of times around the wheelbarrow and then I headed up the tree. I looked down to see Teebo.

"Hey, Teebo, where did you go?" I couldn't see him anywhere.

"Teebo, I know you're here somewhere."

I turned just in time to see Teebo swat at my back. He got me.

"You're it!" He hollered as he jumped to the ground. I leaped down and chased him. I think I got close to him once or twice, but I never could catch him. I began slowing down. I let my tongue hang out the side of my mouth. Heaving and panting, I convinced Teebo that I was tired. He crouched down behind the monkey grass and swatted at the long green blades.

"What's the matter slowpoke? Are you tired?"

As I walked closer to Teebo, I let my legs drag along the ground.

"Yeah," I said. "You're just too fast for me." When I knew I was close enough, I pounced on him.

"Ha, ha, you thought I was tired." I grabbed hold of his tail with my paws. My claws weren't out because I was only playing with him. We rolled over and over each other in the tall monkey grass.

"You're it."

"No, you're it."

"Nope, you are."

Finally we were both laughing so hard we couldn't talk. It didn't matter who was it anymore.

"Kikki, you're my best friend even if you are a girl and don't have a tail."

He liked to tease me about being a girl and not having a tail. It didn't bother me too much because it was Teebo who saved my life. I actually felt pretty lucky to have any of my tail left at all. I knew Teebo loved me anyway.

"You know," said Teebo, "I'll never forget the way Max cried and whimpered all the way to his doghouse. I'm sure he learned his lesson after we got through with him."

"Yeah, but I don't think we'll ever use his yard as a shortcut to the meadow again."

We strolled over to the soft dry dirt beneath the holly bush. We made ourselves comfortable and got ready to take our afternoon nap. I glanced over at the small hole in Teebo's rotting wood fence where the little accident had happened. A mist clouded my eyes as I remembered.

That day had been pretty and bright. Teebo and I had decided to go to the meadow to chase butterflies. The meadow was one of our favorite places to chase them because they liked to linger around the wildflowers. We had to be careful in the field because the cows lived there. A big fence surrounded the meadow to keep the huge beasts from running away. We discovered that the best place to chase the butterflies was near the pond where the cows drank. It was like the one in Teebo's yard, only a lot bigger. The water wasn't as pretty and clear either. It was mostly green and slimy around the edges. Teebo and I would search the wildflowers that grew thick near the pond. That day, we never got there.

We had decided to take a shortcut through the hole in Teebo's fence. Teebo went first. He was quiet and fast as he passed the clearing between Max's doghouse and the People house. When he reached the fence on the other side of Max's yard, he waved his paw for me to hurry.

"The coast is clear. I think Max is inside the People house," he yelled. "Come on!"

I made it to the middle of the yard when the nasty mean dog leaped out of his doghouse and started chasing me. I pulled some of my moves on him, but when I got back to the hole in the fence I didn't quite make it all the way through. Max tried to eat me in one gulp, but I managed to wiggle my body through the hole. My tail was another story. Max bit down on it. He started pulling on it, trying to drag me back through the hole. He tugged and pulled. I clawed at the wood. Terrified, I grabbed for whatever I could get my paws on. I clung to anything and everything. I even dug my nails down deep in the dirt, hoping to keep the rest of my body from ending up in Max's smelly mouth. I knew he was going to hurt me real bad. I struggled to pull away from him. As I felt Max's teeth starting to sink into my back leg, Teebo leaped out of nowhere, right onto Max's head. He dug his claws so deep into Max's nose that Max tucked his tail in and cried all the way to his doghouse. Teebo saved my life. When I looked back, my tail was gone. It hurt bad, but I was so happy to be alive it didn't really matter much.

Teebo rolled over and thumped my nose with his paw. It woke me out of my daydream.

We lay there awake for a long time soaking up the last of the day's sunshine.

"Kikki, kitty, come eat."

"I guess I'd better go," I said. "Carol's got my supper ready."

"Okay," said Teebo, "but don't forget that we're going to Miss Fern's for milk tomorrow."

"I won't. I never forget milk day at Fern's. See you tomorrow."

Fern was the sweetest lady in our neighborhood. Well, next to Carol and Teebo's Mama People. Fern loved us a lot. She always put two big bowls full of milk out for us and sometimes she would give us leftover turkey. Fern was old, but she was pretty. She always kept her silver hair in a knot at the back of her head. Her eyes were sparkling and she liked to sing. She really loved me and Teebo. We loved her too.

I leaped and climbed over the gate and headed across the street for home. I was pretty hungry since Teebo and I had done nothing but chase each other all day long. Carol let me in the back door. I veered far away from the sweeper that she had left in the middle of the living room floor. Staying close to the wall I hurried to the kitchen. Carol already had my dinner ready. Sitting on the floor next to the refrigerator was my special green kitty bowl, filled with my favorite food. . . . TUNA.

After I ate, I curled up on the couch next to Carol. She rubbed behind my ears and under my chin. I loved when she scratched under my chin. I purred to let her know I loved her and the attention she was giving me.

CHAPTER 3

I slept all morning in the bay window. Carol had a whole bunch of potted plants there. She had been looking for me all day. The big green leaves made a good hiding place when Carol wanted to throw me outside. The foliage was thick, and she never looked in the window. I wanted to go outside, but not until later. I wanted to wait until the sun was straight overhead, the time when Teebo and I liked to start our day in the sunshine.

"Kikki?" I heard Carol ask herself. "Where is that cat?"

When she went to the bedroom to look under the bed, I sneaked into the dining room.

I crawled under the table and into one of the chairs. Slowly, I stretched my front paws out in front of me and lifted my rump into the air. I figured if I stretched real good like that, Carol would believe I'd been there all day.

"There you are, Kikki, sweet kitty. Have you been hiding in that chair all day? I should have looked there. That was a pretty good hiding place."

Carol picked me up and put me in the wood chair on the front porch. I stood there for a while, looking at the road that ran in front of the house. It was a long gray stretch of street that went as far as I could see both ways. I peered in the direction of Fern's house. It was on the same side of the street as my house, but it was on the next block. I could see her mailbox but not the flowers and hummingbirds on it. Fern had painted it herself. Her house was the third house on that block. Kylie, the neighborhood terror, lived next door to Fern's. A big elm tree stood in the middle of the little girl's yard. On the corner was the Williamses' two-story home. It was the prettiest one on the block. Their big porch was painted forest green, and the yard was splashed with colorful flowers.

I looked over at Carol as she watered her outside plants. When she turned toward me and the door, I stretched once more just to continue my innocent look. When Carol went inside, I sped across the street and shot through the wooden gate into Teebo's yard.

"Hey, Kikki, you ready to head to Fern's?"

"Yeah, I'm craving milk."

The two of us went back across the street to my house, then headed to Fern's. The sun warmed the sidewalk, so we stayed on it. It was nice to have warm paws. When we passed the Williamses' house, we had to check their flowers. Mrs. Williams always kept her garden nice and pretty. Growing near the front of the house were giant canna plants. They were bright orange and yellow. Teebo and I liked to hide from each other under the broad leaves. It was like a jungle under there—moist, dark, and full of all kinds of living critters. We chased a few bugs and some tiny green frogs. When we got bored, we trotted back to the sidewalk and headed to Fern's.

I knew Teebo wasn't watching where he was

going because he ran over me when I stopped. My ears flattened close against my head as I lowered my body to the concrete. The fur on my back stood up stiff.

"What's the matter, Kikki? Why did you stop all of a sudden?"

"Let's take the long way. I don't want to go near little Kylie's house. You know she's probably watching for us."

"She won't get us. We're too fast. Anyway, I don't see her and . . ."

I stopped again.

"There she is. I told you she'd be watching for us."

We both gritted our teeth when we saw her. Kylie's pudgy little nose was turned up at the end. She had round cheeks the color of Carol's roses, and she always wore a fluffy dress with lace around the bottom. She twisted at the waist when she walked so that her skirt would flip behind her.

We hunkered down as close to the ground as we could. My body was shaking so hard Teebo had to hold on to me to keep me from bouncing away.

Just the thought of her sent chills through me. Kylie got us once before, and we vowed never to let her catch us again.

When she turned away, we raced to the side of the house. We hid behind the big, red clay planter in the Williamses' front yard and watched as Kylie's pigtails flopped and bounced at the back of her head.

"Oh no! Look, she's got one."

Kylie carried a white, fluffy kitten to the bottom of the elm tree. When she got to the old rickety ladder leading up to her tree house, she put the cat in her bright pink backpack and zipped it shut.

"Poor thing." Teebo sighed. "She's taking him . . . up there."

"Shhh," I hissed. "Just be thankful it's not you. Now be quiet so she doesn't find us."

Kylie tossed the backpack (and the poor kitty) over one shoulder and clumsily made her way up the ladder. Her tree house was all wood and had a window on each side. She had used pieces of her dad's old orange hunting jacket to dress up the windows. A little table was inside. The tablecloth was made from her old pink sheets. From where we were, we could see her table lined with tiny plastic cups. The first time she caught us, Teebo and I thought there would be milk in those cups. There wasn't! The cups really held something she called tea. The brown liquid tasted like dirty, gritty water. It was GROSS!

"I hope he doesn't try it," said Teebo.

"Yeah, but if he does—we'll know. He'll be spitting and coughing like we did. The kitten might even throw up like you did when you tried that stuff."

I laughed, remembering. Teebo shoved me hard with his shoulder.

"You're just jealous." He laughed. "You didn't get as much TEEEEEEA as I did."

The way he said *tea* made me laugh even harder.

"Don't look now," I said. "She's holding the pink doll dress."

I could see Teebo tense up. His shoulders were tight and the fur on his back stood on end. I was still laughing. Teebo wasn't. He hated this part, worst of all. Last time she caught us, Kylie dressed *him* like a girl. We managed to escape to the meadow before she took the dress off him.

Teebo climbed back and forth under the barbed wire fence surrounding the meadow. He must have run under that fence at least fifteen times trying to snag the dress to pull it off. Finally he was lucky. The dress caught on the barbed wire. There was a terrible struggle, but Teebo managed to wiggle out of the frilly thing.

"You looked like a butterfly wiggling out of a cocoon." I teased. "You were so pretty in that little dress."

Teebo took a swat at me. He missed on purpose and we both laughed. Fact was, we were laughing too hard to notice that Kylie had come down out of the tree and was sneaking up on us.

"Run, Kikki," I heard Teebo scream. "She's right behind you."

I really didn't have a chance. I ran, but I found myself cornered up against her redbrick house. Frantically, my claws sprang out. I leaped up onto the bricks, trying to climb to safety. My claws wouldn't hold in the hard

brick. I slid back to the ground. It was hope-
less; I was going nowhere. All I could do was
curl myself into a little ball and hope she
would go away.

Then . . . I heard the most terrible sound I
had ever heard in my entire life!

A shrill, screeching noise came from behind
Kylie's tree. She turned away from me and covered her ears. In the blink of an eye, I took off
across her yard to Miss Fern's. Not only did I
need to get away from Kylie, I needed to get
away from that awful noise.

When I got to Fern's, I realized Teebo wasn't
there yet. I looked under the porch to see if he
was hiding. My friend was nowhere to be seen.

CHAPTER 4

Teebo, where are you?" I yelled frantically.

I turned when I heard the sound of feet sliding toward me on the wood planks of the porch.

"Teebo, I thought she grabbed you up. I was worried. Did you hear that awful noise?"

"Yeah, that was me."

"You made that noise on purpose?"

"It worked, didn't it?"

"Yeah, but how did you do it? I mean, I don't know how that horrible sound could have come from you."

Teebo gave me his sheepish grin. "It was easy," he said. "I just started with the meow I give my Mama People and made it louder and higher. I was trying to sound like the sirens on the fire trucks that zoom down the street. Not bad, huh?"

"Well, you scared me. I'm sure Kylie was scared too. She turned and ducked when she heard it, as if a spaceship was going to land on her head or something."

Teebo chuckled as I described Kylie's worried expression. I tried to show him the way her face scrunched up to look like a prune.

Fern must have heard us on the porch because she came out with two big bowls of milk.

"Hello, you two," she said.

As usual, her hair was pulled back into a knot. We nuzzled her legs with our heads to say hi. Her stockings were baggy around her ankles. She put the milk down and sat in her porch swing to watch us lap up every last drop. When she saw we were through, she opened the bag of leftover turkey.

"A piece for you and a piece for you," she said. "Now don't fuss. There's plenty for both of you."

We never fought over the turkey, but sometimes she would drop a piece right between us and we'd go for it at the same time. Miss Fern didn't want anyone fighting. She was so sweet, I guess she couldn't stand to hear arguing or fussing.

When all the turkey was gone, I curled up by Miss Fern's feet. Today was Teebo's turn to take a nap on the soft blue blanket next to her on the swing. She sang about being somewhere over the rainbow as she worked on one of her beautiful blankets. She told us one time that she liked to make them for her friends. She was usually working on a new one every other time we came over. Today, it was a light pink one. Her knitting needles clicked together as she worked, row by row. She left the yarn on the ground by her feet.

"This one," she said, "is for my great-granddaughter. She'll be born this fall, in November."

Fern's eyes seemed to sparkle even more than normal. Her knitting needles clicked faster and faster as she told us about her great-granddaughter.

"I think she'll have my brown eyes," she said, "and maybe she'll have my complexion."

Fern said she always got compliments on her skin. It was milky white and smooth, except for a few wrinkles.

"I've always taken good care of my skin. I stayed out of the sun when I was younger and I always drink at least one glass of milk a day," she said as she worked faster on the blanket.

She began humming.

Reaching out with my paw, I swatted a ball of green yarn in her big brown knitting basket. For a while, I watched as it wobbled around in the basket. With Fern's humming and the continuous clicking of her needles, I found myself getting very tired. My eyes were heavy and eventually I drifted off to sleep.

HOOOONNNNNKKKK!

My eyes flashed open and I quickly jumped to my feet. I turned to look at the big white Cadillac that was making all the noise on the street.

"Kylie, get down out of that tree and in the car this second. I'm going to have to tell your father how you've been behaving today. Just wait till he gets home. Now hurry up and get in this car."

Kylie grinned down at her mother and climbed higher in the tree. Her eyes were little squinty slits.

"Come get me," she said.

Her mother honked the horn again. "Put that cat down and climb down from the tree. You're going to make me late for my women's club meeting."

I looked up at Teebo on the porch swing. He had curled himself into a ball and was snuggled up close to Miss Fern. Not once did he take his eyes from Kylie, who was lurking in the tree only one yard away.

After what seemed like a long time, Kylie climbed down from the tree and got in the car. The white Cadillac zoomed away.

Fern reached down to give me a nice scratch behind the ears. At the same time, she scratched Teebo's neck.

"I've got to go in now and take my afternoon nap. You two be good and don't forget to come see me again."

Fern slowly pushed herself up from the

swing, then opened the creaky front door and went inside.

"Let's go save poor White Kitty," I said as we stretched out our legs. "He's probably still shaking up there in that tree. Poor thing didn't have a fighting chance against Kylie."

Side by side, we leaped off the porch and cautiously made our way toward Kylie's yard. At the base of the tree, we stopped, took a quick look to make sure the white Cadillac was nowhere in sight, then looked back up the tree.

"Trunk or ladder?" Teebo asked.

I shrugged my fur. "Trunk's faster," I answered.

Teebo gave a quick nod and started up the tree. I followed him to where the trunk split, forking out in opposite directions. The tree house was nestled in the V that the branches made. The ladder went from the ground up to the door of the house. We could reach the doorway from the trunk, but it was easier to stay on the tree and jump in one of the windows.

"Let's take the one to the right," I said.

"Yeah," replied Teebo, "looks like the window on that side might be easier to get in since there aren't any weeds to jump over."

The window on our left side had a cup full of dandelions sitting in it. I guess Kylie thought they were pretty. They just made us sneeze.

The awful smell of cheap perfume made us cringe when we jumped through the window. I think Teebo was having flashbacks because he looked like he was about to be sick.

I ran over to White Kitty in the corner. His backside was wedged into a corner of the house. He was shaking. The pink dress Kylie had put on him was draped over the back of one of her chairs. A box full of doll dresses was under the table, and there were bows scattered throughout the tree house.

"Come on, let's get you out of here before Kylie comes back."

His eyes were opened wide, but he didn't move an inch when I tried to push him toward the door.

"Kylie will be back," I said. "You need to get out of here. Go home to your family."

A small whiny sound came from White Kitty's mouth.

"What did you say?" I asked.

"That girl is mean. She made me drink dirty water and dressed me like a girl. She stinks too."

"I know," I said. "Once you get home, don't ever come around here again. Kylie is the meanest girl in this whole neighborhood. She'll run you down and drag you out of hiding places if she finds you. Avoid her yard at all costs. I don't think she wanders too far from her own house, but she can probably smell you a mile away."

"Come on," Teebo said. "Quit chitchatting and let's go. It feels creepy just being up here."

We coaxed White Kitty to the door. Teebo leaped to the ground. White Kitty was next.

"Jump," I said as the little thing just stood there.

"No way, I'll hurt myself. I can't jump."

"What do you mean you can't jump?" Teebo said. "Haven't you ever jumped out of a tree before?"

"Well, actually, this is my first day to go out of my yard by myself. I've never even been in a tree before."

I gave Teebo a dirty look when he started to giggle. I wanted to giggle too, but I knew if I did, we wouldn't get the kitty out of the tree before Kylie came home.

"Come on, let's try it this way." I turned around backward and showed him how to climb out of the door.

"Just grab the bark with your hind claws and make your way slowly down the tree. That way, you don't have to look to see how far down the ground is. When you get older, you'll be able to jump from the top of this tree. It'll be easy."

White Kitty turned sideways and stuck one of his back feet out the door.

"Good," I praised, "now turn backward and stick your other foot on the bark."

Instead of turning backward, he tried to grab the bark with his front foot. He looked pretty funny—half of him still in the tree house, the other half dangling out, grabbing for the tree. I didn't have time to laugh though.

A big white Cadillac came zooming around the corner and into the driveway.

"Jump," I screamed. "You have to jump now. It's your only chance."

He froze. I nudged him with my head and watched as he landed on the ground next to Teebo. I jumped down after him.

"I did it," he said with a big grin on his face.

"Good job," Teebo and I said in unison.

"Next time, you won't have to be scared," I said, turning just in time to see Kylie running in our direction. Her arms were open wide as she came at us.

"Oh, boy, three beautiful kitties. All for me."

I pushed White Kitty. "Run home. Don't stop, don't turn around, just run until you get home. We'll see you around."

By the time Kylie got within reaching distance, we had scattered. Teebo and I ran one way while White Kitty raced toward his home. Kylie chased him down the sidewalk. We watched from the Williamses' house as she ran behind him. We wanted White Kitty to make it home safely. Kylie gave up when she fell on the sidewalk. She started screaming and crying.

"Oh, I broke my leg. Oh, I'm going to lose all my blood. Somebody please help."

Kylie's mom ran out of the house and to her side.

"My poor baby." She whined. "What have you done?"

When Kylie finally quit crying, all she had was a tiny scratch on her knee. It was hardly bleeding. Her dress had a small tear in it that her mom was worried about.

"I told you not to wear that dress to play in. Now do you see why? Look, you got it dirty."

Kylie's bottom lip quivered as she looked at the tiny hole.

"I ruined my favorite dress," she said as she began screaming and crying again. Her mom carried her back to the house.

"Come on, let's go home," Teebo said. "I've had enough excitement for one day."

CHAPTER 5

We sneaked inside Teebo's front door when his Mama People opened it. She was carrying a large box and didn't even notice we were there. Even if she did notice, she liked me, so she didn't really mind if I was in her house.

"Teebo, what's with all these boxes?"

"I think they're putting more stuff in the attic and the garage. Daddy always says Mama's got too much junk in this little house. So, every once in a while, they'll box things up and store them in the attic or garage. I don't know why they can't just throw stuff out."

We made a path through the boxes in the living room to the bathroom. Running from Kylie had made us pretty thirsty, so we took turns lapping up the water that was by the sink. For some reason, Teebo's Mama People put water in a cup and kept it by the bathroom sink. I guess it was so she would remember to fill it up for him. When we got through drinking, we jumped on the big water bed. We liked jumping on it because it rocked us up and down and side to side.

"You wanna play hide-and-seek in the house?" asked Teebo.

"Sure, but you have to be it first."

Teebo gave me a pretend frown. "Fine, go hide, but you have to stay in the house." Teebo turned and shoved his head under a pillow. "One, two, three . . ."

I tore through the house and into the kitchen. I noticed more boxes on the counter. I ran back to the living room and decided to hide in one of the really big ones there. Stepping back from the box, I made a running leap and landed at the bottom of the deep container. It was dark and empty except for Teebo's catnip mouse. I curled up in a ball and waited. I held my breath when I heard someone prowling around outside my box. Suddenly I felt it being lifted with me in it.

"No, don't put me in the attic," I cried. "There are scary things up there. Don't make me go up there, please."

"Oh, Kikki, I didn't know you were here. You silly cat, what are doing in that box? Get out of there. Go play somewhere else." She turned the big thing sideways so I could get out easily.

I took off for the kitchen, so I could hide in the boxes on the countertop. Hopping up, I was cautious not to step on the stove. I burned myself once before and was always careful where I was walking. I jumped into the little box near the kitchen sink. It wasn't empty like the other one. Silver spoons, forks, and knives lined the bottom. Plastic containers were stacked on top. I wondered what good they would do in the attic. Why was all this stuff boxed up?

I froze when I heard a whiffing sound outside. Glancing up at the top of the box, I saw Teebo looking down at me. His face was all grin, from one fuzzy ear to the other.

"Where are you going to go, Kikki?" he asked as his paw reached down into the box.

"Teebo, you know that box in the living room? It's got your favorite catnip toy in it, the one that only has one eye because you chewed off the other one."

When Teebo turned toward the living room I flew out of the box and zoomed down the hallway. I hid under the bed in the bedroom. I could see Teebo's legs as he walked through the doorway. He stopped, then ran to the far side of the bed. Quietly, I crawled out and went to the living room, to my favorite hiding place. The bookshelves were the best place in the house to hide. They had big pictures and books I could hide behind. When I jumped up, I was surprised to find there was nothing on the lower shelves. All the pictures were gone. There were no books either. Not even one figurine stood on the shelf. Nothing. I had to jump really high to get to the top self. There was nothing on it either, but at least Teebo would have to work pretty hard to find me. I stayed there for a long time. Finally I heard Teebo prowling around beneath me.

"Kikki, come out. Where are you?"

I peered down from the shelf. He happened to look up at me as I did.

"There you are."

"It's about time you found me. I've been up here a long time. I didn't have anything to hide behind on the lower shelves. All the pictures and books are gone," I said.

"Yeah, I noticed my favorite scratch post is in one of those boxes. The food bowl I used when I was a kitten is also in there. I even found some of the toys I used to play with. Come down and look. You'll like some of this stuff."

I hopped down off the shelf and followed Teebo to the boxes in the corner of the living room. He started pulling stuff out of them. I helped.

"Look, is this yours?" I asked. I pulled out a red ball with a tiny bell stuffed inside. We batted it around the living room a couple of times. When it rolled under the couch, we decided to play with something else.

Teebo and I pulled out some stuffed animals and a few catnip toys. It was fun to string them out all over the house. We hid them from each other. I put a few in the bathtub because I knew Teebo would be afraid to go near it.

Teebo hated the bathtub. He had fleas one time, so his Mama had to give him a bath. Teebo thought she was trying to drown him. Since then he was afraid to go near the thing.

Some things I hid in the closet. They would be easy for him to find since nothing else was in there. I guess they had that stuff in boxes too. They sure were putting a lot of things in the attic this year.

"You two get out of here. You're making a mess." Teebo's Mama People squealed when she realized we were playing with all his old toys. She gently scooted us out the back door with her foot.

"Go play outside for a while."

"They sure are boxing up a lot of stuff this year." I said to Teebo.

"Yeah, but they do that every year. I'm just curious about all my toys. I thought they put my bowl in the attic years ago. Maybe they're just putting that stuff in the garage to make room in the attic for other things."

"Yeah," I agreed. "I bet that's what they're doing."

I could hear Carol calling my name. "Kikki, it's supper time. Come eat."

"I'll see you tomorrow, Teebo. Maybe we can go to the meadow and chase butterflies."

"That's a good idea. We haven't done that in a long time. Try to come over early so we can go see Fern in the afternoon."

"I will. I'm sure Carol will let me outside early if I let her find me. I'll see you in the morning."

I waved bye to Teebo and headed home. My stomach jumped with excitement. We hadn't been to the meadow in a long time and I was looking forward to chasing butterflies.

CHAPTER 6

"Mee-ooout! Mee-ooout!"

No matter how much I cried or how much I told her "Me out," Carol wouldn't open the door for me the next morning. I raced back to the window where I could see the big truck and Teebo's people heaving boxes into the back. They were carrying tables, lamps, the couch, and even Teebo's favorite chair. I wasn't sure what was happening, but I knew I had to talk to Teebo as soon as I could. As I turned back around, I could hear Carol rustle the trash sacks in the kitchen.

Nestling between the wall and Carol's shoes, I waited. With her hands full of trash bags, she opened the door. I darted outside.

"Get back here, Kikki," Carol yelled as the trash bags fell to the ground. But she was too late. I raced across the street, around the truck, and hid under Teebo's porch.

"Kikki, here, kitty, kitty, kitty," I heard Carol yell. Any normal day, I would go to her when she called, but not today. I had to find out what all the commotion was about.

"Teebo, buddy, where are you?" I meowed.

I could barely hear his faint cries.

"I'm in the car in the garage," he wailed.

Cautiously, I crawled out from my hiding place and ran to the sidewalk. Then I flew into the garage.

"What's going on?" I cried. "Why are you in the car? What's with the big truck out front?"

Teebo turned away, trying to hide his tears. "We're moving to the mountains. My people are excited, but I'm scared and sad. I don't want to go, I want to stay here."

"But we were supposed to go to the meadow today. You told me not to forget." I hopped onto the back of the car. Teebo was on the passenger side with the window rolled down a little bit.

"I know," said Teebo. "I just found out today. I knew they were up to something because they were packing so much stuff. I never thought we'd have to move."

I jumped onto the roof and tried to reach the handle to open Teebo's door. It was farther away than I thought. I just couldn't get hold of it no matter how far I stretched. I ran to the driver's side to see if I could get to Teebo that way. The window wasn't down enough for me to get in to help him or for him to escape.

"Teebo, I'm going to get you out, don't worry."

I slid down the windshield and onto the hood of the red car. Looking in through the front, I could see all the boxes in the backseat. Teebo's scratch post was stuffed on the floor.

"I'll get you out," I said. "We're going to the meadow and Miss Fern's, whether your people like it or not."

I tried everything to free Teebo, but there was nothing I could do. The handle was too far away for me to reach, and the window was only open a little bit.

"I'll pretend like I'm getting in on the passenger's side." I heard the Daddy People say. "You know Teebo will try to get out. He always does when we take him to the vet for shots. Well, when he runs to my door, you get in real quick and grab him. I'll get in once you've got a good hold of him."

The Mama People grinned. "Sounds like a good plan to me. Let's go."

They headed for the car.

"Teebo, go to the driver's side, they're trying to trick you. Don't fall for it," I yelled.

It was too late. Teebo didn't hear a word I said. As the Daddy People opened the door, Teebo darted for the passenger door. I watched helplessly as the Mama People yanked her door open, jumped in, and grabbed him. She held him close to her body. Daddy People got in.

I was scared and nervous, but I ran to the car and jumped back up on the roof.

I peeked in the window. "Don't go. You can't leave me after all we've been through," I whimpered. "Especially after you saved my life."

"I just wish I could have gotten there sooner. Your tail was so beautiful."

"But you saved my life. If you leave, I can never repay you. Anyway, I'm starting to like the cute little stub I have." I managed to let out a small giggle.

"You take care of yourself, Kikki. Everything will be all right."

I gave Teebo a half smile.

Teebo stood in the Daddy People's lap and reached a paw out the window. I touched his paw with mine.

"I love you," we said at the same time.

When the Mama People started the engine, I slid down the windshield and leaped to the ground. The car backed out of the driveway and into the road. I walked beside it, careful to stay away from the big black tires. As I watched, I could see Teebo sitting in the back window. He waved a paw.

"Good-bye, I love you."

"I love you too." I howled. They sped away.

I don't know if my friend ever heard me over the loud roar of the motor.

When I could no longer see the car, I

walked to the back. Teebo's backyard was full of memories. The thought of this yard without him . . . well, it made me sad. I would never get to play with Teebo again. My best friend—in the whole wide world—was gone . . . forever.

For a long time, I stood there, staring at the oak tree. I looked down at the ground. I felt so sad and empty inside, I hurt.

When I looked back up at the tree, a tender smile tugged at my whiskers. Teebo was so much fun. As I watched the tree, I could almost see the day Teebo chased Mama Squirrel onto the tin shed.

It had been a chilly day outside, and like most, we'd been playing hide-and-seek. When it was his turn to hide, Teebo decided to chase Mama Squirrel instead. She had been pestering him all afternoon. She chattered, scolded, and called Teebo names.

"Back off!" He'd hissed at her. "If you don't quit, I'll . . ."

"You'll what?" she said.

"That's it." Teebo snarled.

Teebo took off after her. She jumped from the tree. He chased her through the yard. I tried to help him. I headed her off from the tree when she got close. She finally climbed the fence to Max's yard, but when she started to jump for the tree, Teebo was already there. She ended up on the silver shed. Once she was up there, our work was done. The rest was up to the shed.

We got a good laugh as we watched her trying to run. She was going nowhere. The tin roof under her feet wouldn't let her go any place. Her legs were flying in every direction. Teebo was laughing and yelling to her.

"I told you not to mess with me."

"Come on, Teebo." I meowed. "She's learned her lesson." As soon as we left, she quit running. As soon as she quit running, she slid off the roof and raced home.

The sound of rustling grass startled me.

"There you are. Oh, you're going to miss Teebo and his family, aren't you? I'm going to miss them too," Carol said.

I let my head hang low to the ground. Carol picked me up and gave me a good long hug.

"Don't you worry, sweet kitty, I'll take care of you. You won't be lonely."

The hug made me feel a little better, but I was still hurting really bad. What was I going to do without my best friend?

CHAPTER 7

All week long, I moped around the house.

"Honey, Kikki must be sick. Her motor's not running," I heard Carol say.

I tried to purr for Carol, but a tiny sound was all I could muster.

By Saturday I decided it was time to stop feeling sorry for myself. I was going to find a new best friend! Carol opened the front door for me, and I began prancing up the street. I didn't really know where to start looking. To be honest, I never really had to look for a friend before. When Teebo moved in across the street, he immediately came to my house and introduced himself. He asked if I wanted to be his best friend and I said yes. At that time I didn't know what a best friend was, but it sounded really nice, so I agreed. Ever since that day, we were buddies.

When I got to the Williamses' house, I crossed the street. I didn't want to go by Kylie's house, and I figured I would stop by Fern's on the way home.

In the yard across from Fern's, I noticed a beautiful tabby cat. She was prissing around the bushes that were up next to the house. This is my chance, I thought to myself. I walked up next to her. I gave her my best smile.

"Hi, my name is Kikki. What's your name?"

She arched her back. "My goodness, where is your tail?" She hissed. "Scram, I don't have time for silly little games."

She walked into the garden where her new-born kittens were sleeping. Curling up next to them, she glared at me.

"Go away, you'll scare my babies."

"How rude." I huffed as I turned away from her.

I left her house quickly and stopped at the

next one. A young cat leaped out from behind a bush.

"Howdy," he said. "Where's your tail? Huh? Huh? Why don't you have a tail? You're a cat aren't you?"

He moved from one side of me to the other, talking nonstop. He never even gave me a chance to answer any of his questions.

"Do you ever stop talking?" I asked.

"Oh, well, I like to talk. I guess I always have a lot to say. You want me to tell you a story?"

Before I could say no, he started talking about the time he chased a rabbit and the rabbit turned and chased him. I didn't hear the whole story because I was trying to get away. I had already decided I couldn't be friends with someone who never let me talk. It also made me sad that he was so concerned about my tail. What was the big deal?

I walked a little way down an alley between the tabby's house and the talker's house. Two alley cats stared at me as I passed the Dumpsters.

"Hey, look at stumpy," they whispered.

"Hey, you. Yeah, you bobtailed kitty."

I ignored them. Without a second thought, I turned away from them and went back to where I had come from.

"What's the matter? Cat got your tail? Ur, uh, I mean tongue?"

They began laughing. The bigger one fell to the ground and began rolling around. He covered his stomach with his paws as the laughter became uncontrollable. I swallowed the lump that had formed in my throat. I'm never going to find a friend. No one likes a cat without a tail. I guess I just look weird.

I was getting frustrated, but I remembered one more place I could look for a friend. Walking quickly, I went up to the big stone house I had seen White Kitty run to. He seemed really nice. He was young, but his personality seemed sweet and he didn't talk too much. I prowled around in his front yard. It was kind of like playing hide-and-seek, because I had to check all the places I thought I could find him. If he was anything like Teebo, it would take a long time.

"White Kitty, where are you? Do you live here?"

I looked under the porch. It was dark and damp under there. It wasn't like under Teebo's porch, where the light would shine through the wood lattice around it. It was scary under this porch. I backed out of it as fast as I could, convinced that White Kitty wouldn't dare go under there. Not unless he had to. I stepped carefully amongst the flowers that lined the sidewalk up to the house. The ground was soft and wet. I didn't like to have muddy feet. Peeking around the corner, I decided either White Kitty didn't live here or he was inside. Maybe Kylie had scared him so bad he would never come out again.

I gave up and headed back home.

I decided to stop at Miss Fern's. She could cheer me up. Miss Fern didn't care that my tail was missing and she would bring out a special saucer of milk for me. I wanted her to be my best friend. I knew that would be impossible. She wasn't a cat.

Miss Fern greeted me on the porch. "Hi, kitty. Where's your friend today?"

I rubbed my head against her legs as she talked. Her sweet voice always made me feel good, even if I was having a bad day. I drank the milk and had a few pieces of turkey. Miss Fern sat in the porch swing, rocking back and forth. She was still working on her great-granddaughter's baby blanket. It was quite a bit bigger than when she first told me and Teebo about it. I figured she was nearly done, because the blanket was big enough to cover a baby. When I finished the milk, she invited me to sit in the swing with her. I leaped on the big fluffy blanket she laid out for me. It was one she had made specially for Teebo and me when we started coming to see her regularly. With my claws, I dug in—one foot then the other—until the blanket was just like I wanted it. I took a short nap as Miss Fern rubbed the back of my neck. Her touch was soft and gentle like Carol's. For a short time, I forgot about the lonely, sad feeling that I'd had deep down in my stomach. I forgot how much I missed Teebo and how badly I wanted to find a new friend.

I was tired, so I went back to my own yard. Carol was digging in her roses. The loose dirt felt cool when I plopped down in it. Carol patted my head.

"Come on, Kikki, let's go inside and have supper."

I wasn't hungry, but I followed her anyway. I curled up on the couch, buried my head under my paw, and cried. I'll never find a friend, I thought. Never.

CHAPTER 8

The afternoon sun felt good on my back.
Stretching, I peered out the window. Move-
ment across the street caught my eye. A big
truck pulled into the driveway.

I sprang to my feet.

"Teebo's home!" I yowled.

Eyes wide, I watched for my friend as the
people opened the truck door. *Those aren't
Teebo's people,* I thought as I got a better look
at them.

My shoulders slumped. Disappointed, I lay
back down.

My chest just touched the windowsill when
a car pulled into the driveway. A woman got

out, then reached back into the car and took something out. She held it in her arms.

I saw a long tail. Instantly, I sprang to my feet again. When she turned, I saw . . . what was it . . . yes. Yes! It was a cat!

In the blink of an eye, I leaped over the plants, raced across the room, and slid to a stop at the back door.

"Mee-ooout!" I yelled.

As usual, Carol just stood there looking at me. I made a big circle around the kitchen. This time, when I slid to a stop at the back door, I waited too long. My nose bumped the wood.

"Mee-ooout!"

Frowning down at me, Carol opened the door. The screen wasn't quite shut, so I squeezed through the narrow crack and raced around to the front yard. After looking both ways, I bounded across the street.

By the time I got to Teebo's yard, the woman was at the back gate. A man people stood there with her.

"You get the babies put up?" she asked.

He nodded.

"Yeah. It wasn't easy, but I got all of them in the backyard."

She motioned at the gate. He opened it, just a bit, and she put the cat down. When he hesitated at the gate, she nudged him inside with her foot. The man shut the gate. Smiling, they both walked back to the front yard.

I waited until they were out of the way, then raced to the gate.

"Hello," I called. "Are you still here?"

No one answered. The crack in the old wood gate was barely wide enough for me to squeeze my head through. I had to wiggle and shove and strain to get inside. Once there, I looked around for the cat I had seen.

The pansies in the garden next to the porch were shriveled and the monkey grass looked dry and brown. No one had been taking care of Teebo's beautiful yard. It was a mess. Even the pond looked bad. It was beginning to look like the one in the meadow that the cows drank from. There was very little water in it and what was left was green. The big oak tree still looked the same, but the bushes that were between the tree and the silver shed were beginning to wilt. The shed was empty and the door swung back and forth with the wind.

"Hello," I called again. I walked to the middle of the yard. "Where are you? Your name is Charlie, isn't it? That's what the woman called you. Where are you, Charlie?"

Suddenly I felt something on the back of my neck. It made my fur tingle. There was a wet feeling on my ears. Something was breathing on me.

Ever so slowly, I turned. Three pair of green dog eyes glared down at me.

My heart stopped. My legs quivered so much I thought they were going to fold up under me.

"Hi!" The first one barked.

"Come here, kitty," the second one yipped.

I didn't wait to hear what the third one had to say because I was already headed for the big oak tree in the corner of the yard. My claws tore at the bark. I felt the warm breath again on the back of my neck and paws.

I was far out on one of the smaller limbs when I finally stopped running. It was a narrow limb. It bent under my weight. Ever so carefully, I turned around.

"Leave me alone." I pleaded.

The smallest one jumped up with his front paws on the tree trunk.

"I'm Morris, this is my sister, Doris, and my brother, Boris." He smiled and wagged his tail. "Come play with us."

The one called Boris and his sister, Doris, were huge. The skin on their necks and faces was kind of wrinkled and their paws were nearly the size of Carol's feet. They reminded me of the cows that grazed in the meadow where Teebo and I chased butterflies. Even though we sensed the cows were gentle, we were careful to stay away from the big ugly creatures. Even if they didn't mean to—if they accidentally stepped on us, we would be goners.

Doris and Boris looked like twins. Only Doris was a little smaller and her fur was dark brown with tan spots. Her tongue always seemed to stick out the side of her mouth.

"Please come down and play," the little one yipped.

"No way." I hissed. "You think I'm nuts? You'll eat me for supper! I'm staying up here until you leave."

Morris made a loud *whoopf* sound.

"Silly cat, we're not going to eat you. We just want to play."

Morris wasn't as big as Boris and Doris, and he didn't look as smart as they did either. His head was cocked to one side and his ears were big. They stood up straight on top of his head. He didn't look so much like a cow. He looked more like a jackrabbit.

They kept trying to coax me out of the tree, but I wasn't going to budge. As the sky began to turn dark, I could hear Carol yelling:

"Kikki! Here, kitty, kitty, kitty. Come get your supper."

"Carol, save me!" I meowed back. She didn't answer. I meowed louder and louder. No matter how loud I called, she didn't hear me.

"You should come down now and go eat your supper," Doris said. "You can come back later and play. You've been up there a long time."

There was no way I would fall for their tricks. I decided to wait until someone brought Morris, Doris, and Boris their food. I could escape while they were eating.

I waited and waited and waited, but no one ever brought them food. Maybe they eat in the morning, I decided. The thought worried me. I wanted to get home to Carol. I wanted her to pet my head. I wanted to curl up by her feet and feel safe and warm.

Morris walked over and looked up at Doris.

"What's wrong with that cat?" he asked.

She shrugged her ears.

"Don't ask me." Suddenly she smiled. "I know what we can do. I'll get Charlie. He'll convince her to come play with us."

I watched as Doris disappeared into the shed. When she returned, an old gray cat followed close at her heels. I was confused. Why would a cat be that close to those ugly beasts? They were big and scary. A cat wouldn't be caught dead with a bunch of nasty dogs.

"This is Charlie. He's our friend."

"Your friend?"

"Yes." Charlie purred. He rubbed against Boris's leg. "These guys have lived with me since they were very little. I've kept them in line and taught them to love and respect cats. So why don't you come down and play with them? We just moved here. We're all looking for some new friends. It's hard to find friends when you're new to a place."

I wasn't sure I could trust this guy. Why would they want me to play with them? I had no tail. They probably just wanted me to trust them so they could eat me. I did, however, know what Charlie meant about trying to find new friends. Still, I wasn't about to budge from this tree.

When I didn't move, Charlie finally shrugged his ears.

"Fine. Have it your way, cat. Just stay up there 'til you rot. Come on, guys. Let's leave her alone."

They turned to leave.

"Hey, wait. I guess it's okay."

My legs were wobbly and weak. Slowly, branch by branch, I started down the tree. Then . . . there was a cracking sound. The limb beneath my feet gave way.

Until the branch broke—until that very second, I hadn't noticed where I was. The instant I began to fall, I knew. I was on the forbidden branches.

I was . . .

Everything was spinning. I grabbed with my claws. I twisted by stub tail, trying to catch my balance. Nothing helped.

THUD! CRUNCH!

I was . . .

I was in Max's yard.

"Well, well. What have we here?"

The voice was familiar and scary. I struggled to my feet. Max stood over me. Slowly I backed away.

"Please don't eat me! You ate my tail. Wasn't that enough?"

Max licked his lips. Slobbers dripped from his tongue. He moved closer. I backed up. He took another step toward me. I backed right into the corner of the fence.

Squinting his eyes, Max opened his jaws wide enough so that I could see clear down to his ugly tonsils. I closed my eyes. I hoped it would be over quick.

About the time I expected his teeth to crunch down on me, there was a loud CRASH!

My eyes flashed open, just in time to see

wood splinters fly from the wooden fence beside me.

Something brown and fuzzy flew over my head. I blinked, trying to focus my eyes. Whatever it was, it was big. It moved fast too. I blinked again.

Boris was rolling Max like a ball across the yard.

"Don't you ever touch her again!" Boris growled.

Max snapped at him.

"Big mistake, Max!"

Doris and Morris sailed over my head. They charged across the yard, leaped, and landed square in the middle of Max's tummy. Little Morris bit Max's nose as Doris and Boris pinned him to the ground with their paws.

"If you ever come near her again, we'll eat YOU for supper."

Max's whole body was shaking. "Okay. Okay! I'll never bother her again. Please don't eat me."

The three dogs took a step back. The second they did, Max let out a loud yelp and darted for his doghouse.

Morris, Doris, Boris, and I trotted back through the old wooden fence where they had broken the rotten planks to save my life.

Exhausted, I fell asleep. When I woke up, I realized I was cuddled up next to my four new best friends. Morris, Doris, Boris, and Charlie didn't seem to care if I had no tail. In fact, I don't think they noticed until I pointed it out to them.

"I'm too old to play with the dogs anymore," Charlie said. "But I'm glad they have you now."

He stretched out on the porch and watched as I chased my new best friends through the yard.

About the Author

Nikki Wallace heard lots of children's books when she was growing up. Her dad, Bill Wallace, often read manuscripts to the family while he was polishing them for publication.

As a senior in college, Nikki took a creative writing course. One of her assignments was to write the text for a picture book. Jon-Ed Moore, her husband, suggested that she send it to her father's editor, Patricia MacDonald. Ms. MacDonald liked her writing style and suggested that Nikki "make it a little longer."

Nikki and her husband live in Oklahoma City with their rottweilers, Boris and Tasha. At only twenty-four this is her first novel.